EARTH'S ENERGY EXPERIMENTS

COAL ENERGY PROJECTS

Easy Energy Activities for
Future Engineers!

MEGAN BORGERT-SPANIOL

CONSULTING EDITOR, DIANE CRAIG, M.A./READING SPECIALIST

Super Sandcastle

An Imprint of Abdo Publishing
abdopublishing.com

abdopublishing.com

Published by Abdo Publishing, a division of ABDO, PO Box 398166, Minneapolis, Minnesota 55439. Copyright © 2019 by Abdo Consulting Group, Inc. International copyrights reserved in all countries. No part of this book may be reproduced in any form without written permission from the publisher. Super SandCastle™ is a trademark and logo of Abdo Publishing.

Printed in the United States of America, North Mankato, Minnesota
052018
092018

Design and Production: Mighty Media, Inc.
Editor: Liz Salzmann
Cover Photographs: Mighty Media, Inc.; Shutterstock
Interior Photographs: Alamy; iStockphoto; Mighty Media, Inc.; Shutterstock

The following manufacturers/names appearing in this book are trademarks:
Artist's Loft™, Morton®, Pyrex®, Sharpie®

Library of Congress Control Number: 2017961709

Publisher's Cataloging-in-Publication Data
Names: Borgert-Spaniol, Megan, author.
Title: Coal energy projects: Easy energy activities for future engineers! / by Megan Borgert-Spaniol.
Other titles: Easy energy activities for future engineers!
Description: Minneapolis, Minnesota : Abdo Publishing, 2019. | Series: Earth's energy experiments
Identifiers: ISBN 9781532115615 (lib.bdg.) | ISBN 9781532156335 (ebook)
Subjects: LCSH: Fossil fuels--Juvenile literature. | Handicraft--Juvenile literature. | Science projects--Juvenile literature. | Earth sciences--Experiments--Juvenile literature.
Classification: DDC 333.82--dc23

Super SandCastle™ books are created by a team of professional educators, reading specialists, and content developers around five essential components—phonemic awareness, phonics, vocabulary, text comprehension, and fluency—to assist young readers as they develop reading skills and strategies and increase their general knowledge. All books are written, reviewed, and leveled for guided reading and early reading intervention programs for use in shared, guided, and independent reading and writing activities to support a balanced approach to literacy instruction.

TO ADULT HELPERS

The projects in this title are fun and simple. There are just a few things to remember to keep kids safe. Some projects require the use of hot objects. Also, kids may be using messy materials such as glue or paint. Make sure they protect their clothes and work surfaces. Review the projects before starting, and be ready to assist when necessary.

KEY SYMBOL

Watch for this warning symbol in this book. Here is what it means.

HOT!
You will be working with something hot. Get help!

CONTENTS

WHAT IS COAL ENERGY?

Coal energy is energy created by burning coal. Coal is a **fossil fuel**. It forms underground. People mine coal from the ground. The coal is burned to produce heat and electricity.

COAL BETWEEN LAYERS OF DIRT

Coal forms from dead plants. The plants get buried under layers of dirt and rock. This presses on the plants.

It is very hot underground. The heat and pressure turn the plants into coal. This process takes millions of years.

MINED COAL

Coal is a nonrenewable **resource**. This is because it takes so long for new coal to form. It's possible that we could use it up. Experts say the use of coal power will go down in the coming years.

COAL FIRE

COAL MINING AND BURNING

Coal must be removed from the ground before it is burned. This process is called mining. There are two main methods of coal mining. These are surface mining and underground mining.

SURFACE MINING

Surface mining is a way to mine coal that is close to Earth's surface. Miners remove the dirt and rock above the coal. This is an easy and inexpensive way to mine coal. But it destroys the land and animal **habitats**.

UNDERGROUND MINING

Underground mining removes coal from far below Earth's surface. Miners dig deep shafts and work underground. This type of mining can pollute water sources. It is also very **dangerous** for the miners.

BURNING COAL

Most coal is burned in power plants. It powers the **generators** that make electricity. However, this process pollutes the air. This is harmful to humans and the **environment**. Experts look for ways to reduce the pollution from burning coal.

COAL HISTORY

Humans have burned coal for hundreds of years. They used the heat for cooking food and warming homes. And blacksmiths used coal fires to melt metal.

The first **commercial** power plant was completed in 1882. It was on Pearl Street in New York City. The plant burned coal to produce electricity for one square mile (2.6 sq. km). It lit streetlights and lights inside buildings.

PEARL STREET POWER PLANT

JAMES WATT

James Watt was a Scottish inventor. In 1764, Watt was repairing a steam engine. He noticed that it wasted a lot of energy. He invented a new model that fixed this problem. Watt's steam engine increased the need for coal. Steam engines powered many **industries**. And the steam engines were powered by coal!

Today, coal is used for electricity around the world. Coal power plants produce about 30 percent of US electricity. And they produce about 40 percent of the world's electricity!

WATT'S STEAM ENGINE

MATERIALS

Here are some of the materials that you will need for the projects in this book.

BALLOONS

BLACK PEPPER

BOWL

CHOCOLATE CHIP COOKIE

CLEAR PLASTIC CUPS

COFFEE GROUNDS

DRINKING GLASS

FERN FRONDS

FINE SAND

HEAVY PLATE

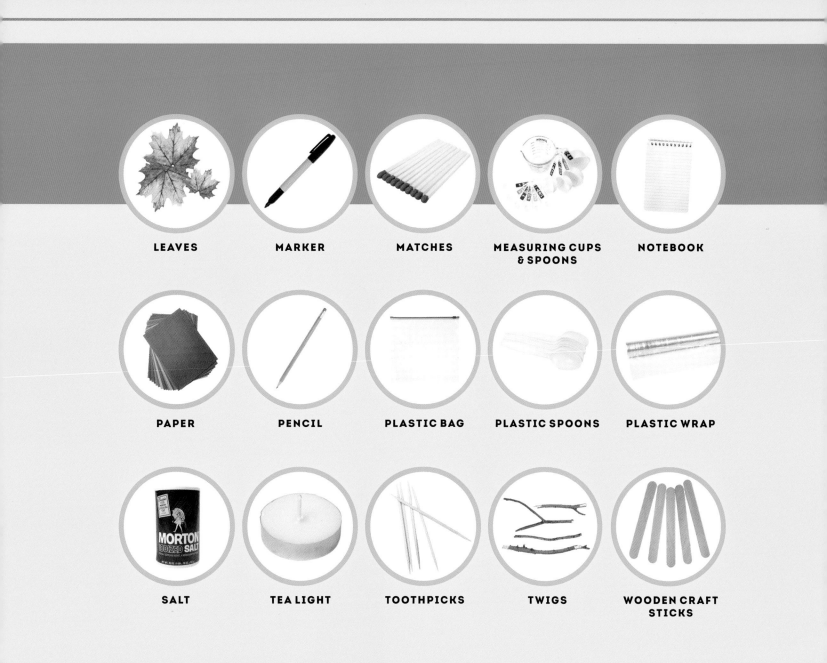

LEAVES

MARKER

MATCHES

MEASURING CUPS
& SPOONS

NOTEBOOK

PAPER

PENCIL

PLASTIC BAG

PLASTIC SPOONS

PLASTIC WRAP

SALT

TEA LIGHT

TOOTHPICKS

TWIGS

WOODEN CRAFT
STICKS

PEAT FORMATION SANDBOX

MATERIALS: plastic container, plastic wrap, ruler, water, fine sand, twigs, leaves, fern fronds, notebook, pencil

Coal is formed over millions of years. It begins as organic matter called peat. This project shows how peat forms.

BEFORE

AFTER

① Line the plastic container with plastic wrap.

② Pour about 3 inches (7.6 cm) of water into the container.

③ Add about 1½ inches of fine sand.

④ Add twigs, leaves, and fern fronds to the container.

⑤ Record in a notebook what the contents of the container look like. Try drawing a picture of it too.

⑥ Place the container in a garage or other large space. Leave it there for two weeks.

Continued on the next page.

7 Observe the container. How have the contents changed? Record your observations in your notebook.

8 Gently add another 1 to 2 inches (2.5 to 5 cm) of sand. What happens?

9 Set the container aside for another two weeks.

10 Carefully pour out the remaining water.

11 Let the contents dry for one week. Observe the contents.

12 Try to remove a sample of the layers. How has the layer of plant life changed over time?

DIGGING DEEPER

Coal formation began about 300 million years ago. Seas flooded forests and created swamps. As the plants died, they were buried under layers of sand and soil. The wet soil trapped carbon from the rotting plants. This created peat. Over time, heat and pressure turned the peat into coal. This process is called carbonization. Today, coal is found in different stages of carbonization. But the energy of plants from millions of years ago is in coal at every stage!

300 MILLION YEARS AGO: SWAMP

100 MILLION YEARS AGO: OCEAN

TODAY: ROCK LAYERS

SAND AND SOIL   PEAT

ROCKS AND SOIL   COAL

CEREAL ROCK LAYERS

MATERIALS: measuring cups & spoons, bowl, chocolate rice cereal, coffee grounds, warm water, 2 clear plastic cups, three other kinds of breakfast cereal, plastic bag, drinking glass, paper, marker

Conditions must be just right for peat to turn into coal. The peat must be exposed to heat and pressure. This happens when peat is buried deep beneath layers of dirt and rock.

1. Put ½ cup of chocolate rice cereal and 2 tablespoons of coffee grounds in a bowl.

2. Stir in 2 tablespoons of warm water.

3. Put some of the mixture in a clear plastic cup. This layer represents peat.

Continued on the next page.

④ Put ½ cup of one of the other cereals in a plastic bag. Seal the bag.

⑤ Use a drinking glass to crush the cereal.

⑥ Pour the crushed cereal into the plastic cup.

⑦ Repeat steps 4 through 6 with the remaining kinds of cereal.

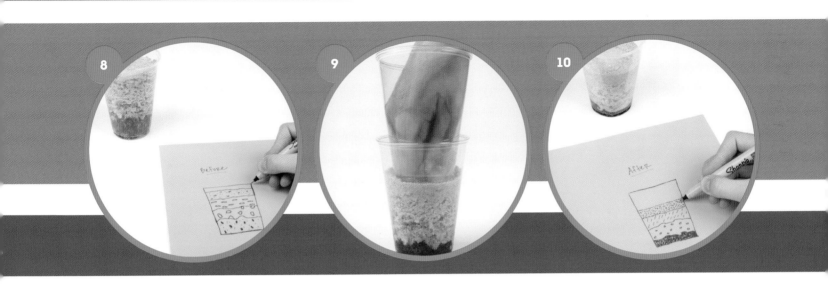

8 Observe the layers. Each layer of cereal represents a different layer of rock. Draw what you see.

9 Place the second plastic cup inside the first one. Place your hand inside the empty cup and push down onto the rock layers.

10 Observe the layers in the cup. Draw what you see. How did the bottom peat layer change? How did the other layers change?

COOKIE MINING

MATERIALS: paper, chocolate chip cookie, marker, plate, toothpicks

Coal is mined from Earth's surface or from deep underground. Miners use different methods and machines for each type of mining. In this project, the chocolate chips represent coal. The rest of the cookie represents the land.

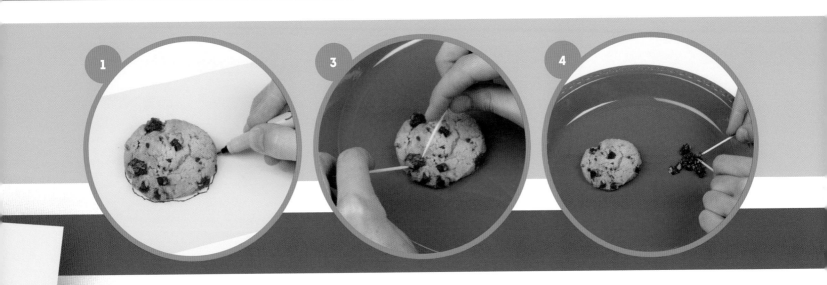

1 Place a cookie on a sheet of paper. Trace the outline of the cookie. This represents the land before mining.

(2) Place the cookie on a plate.

3 Use one or two toothpicks to remove the chocolate chips from the surface of the cookie. Try to keep the rest of the cookie together and only remove the chocolate chips.

4 Place the mined chocolate chips in a pile next to the cookie.

Continued on the next page.

5 Use the toothpicks to remove the chocolate chips inside the cookie. Is it easier or harder to mine these chips compared to the surface chips?

6 Carefully gather the pieces of cookie. Place them back inside the cookie outline.

7 Place the mined chocolate chips in a pile next to the cookie pieces.

8 Observe the cookie and pile of chips. How much has the cookie changed from its original form? This represents how mining changes land.

DIGGING DEEPER

Surface mining removes coal that is less than 200 feet (60 meters) underground. Miners clear away trees, soil, and rock to reach the coal. This process is less costly than underground mining. But it causes great harm to land. The land must be **restored** after mining is finished.

Underground mining removes coal that is deep below Earth's surface. These mines can be 1,000 feet (300 meters) deep! Underground mining is less harmful to the land than surface mining. However, it is much more **dangerous**. Miners can die from toxic gases, explosions, and lack of oxygen.

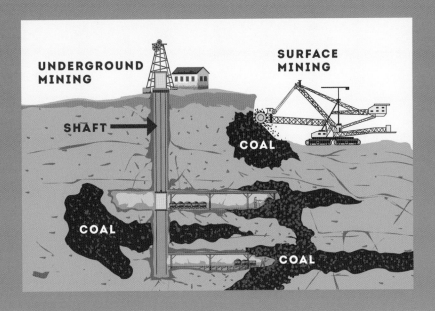

OXYGEN BURN

MATERIALS: tea light, matches, drinking glass, stopwatch, notebook, pencil, heavy plate, 8 wooden craft sticks

Coal power plants pump oxygen into furnaces where coal is burned. This is because coal needs oxygen to burn. The oxygen **reacts** with carbon in the coal. This produces heat energy! You can use a candle to show how oxygen is needed for burning.

① Have an adult help you light a tea light.

② Place a glass over the candle. Start the stopwatch. Stop the watch when the flame goes out. Record the time in a notebook.

③ Light the candle again. Place the glass back over the candle. Then place a heavy plate on top of the glass.

④ Start the stopwatch. Stop the watch when the flame goes out. Record the time in a notebook.

⑤ Place a pile of four craft sticks on each side of the candle. Then light the candle a third time.

⑥ Place the glass over the candle so the glass rests on the craft sticks. The sticks let oxygen enter the glass.

⑦ Start the stopwatch. Stop the watch when the flame goes out. Record the time in a notebook.

⑧ Compare the three times you recorded. What conditions let the flame burn the longest? Do the results reflect the amount of oxygen in the glass?

SALT-AND-PEPPER SOOT COLLECTION

MATERIALS: plate, measuring spoons, salt, black pepper, plastic spoon, stopwatch, felt or wool, rug (optional), sweater (optional), balloon

Burning coal produces gases and smoke. Inside these gases are tiny bits of carbon called soot. Soot pollutes the air. But power plants can trap most soot before it gets into the atmosphere. This project shows how soot is removed from gases using static electricity.

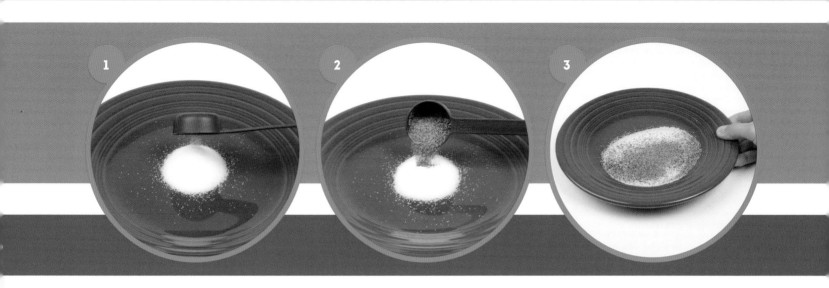

1. Pour 2 tablespoons of salt onto a plate.

2. Add 1 tablespoon of pepper.

3. Gently shake the plate to mix the salt and pepper.

Continued on the next page.

④ Rub the back of a plastic spoon against a piece of felt or wool for 30 seconds.

⑤ Hold the spoon just above the pile of salt and pepper. Move the spoon back and forth. Watch as the pepper separates from the salt and sticks to the spoon!

⑥ Try rubbing the spoon against other materials, such as a rug, a sweater, or even your hair!

⑦ Then try using a balloon instead of a spoon. Which object and material work best to remove the pepper from the salt?

Static electricity is a **positive** or **negative** electric charge on an object. When the object touches an object with the opposite charge, the two objects are **attracted** to each other. Rubbing the spoon against felt gave the spoon a negative charge. The pepper was positively charged. So, the pepper was pulled to the spoon!

Coal power plants use this idea to trap soot. The waste gases pass through a metal screen. This gives the soot in the gases a negative charge. Then the gases flow past positively charged plates. The plates attract the negatively charged soot. The soot collects on the plates instead of escaping into the atmosphere!

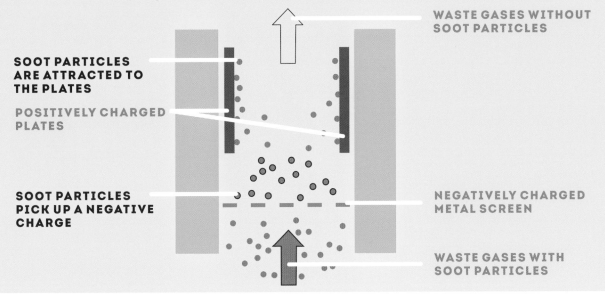

WASTE GASES WITHOUT SOOT PARTICLES

SOOT PARTICLES ARE ATTRACTED TO THE PLATES

POSITIVELY CHARGED PLATES

SOOT PARTICLES PICK UP A NEGATIVE CHARGE

NEGATIVELY CHARGED METAL SCREEN

WASTE GASES WITH SOOT PARTICLES

CONCLUSION

Coal energy comes from burning coal. Burning coal produces heat and electricity. But it also harms the **environment** and causes pollution. Scientists are looking for ways to make coal power cleaner.

QUIZ

1. Coal is a **fossil fuel**. TRUE OR FALSE?

2. What are the two main methods of coal mining?

3. Which invention did James Watt improve?

LEARN MORE ABOUT IT!

You can find out more about coal energy at the library. Or you can ask an adult to help you **research** coal energy on the internet!

Answers: 1. True   2. Surface mining and underground mining   3. Steam engine

GLOSSARY

attract – to cause something to move closer.

commercial – having to do with the buying and selling of goods and services.

dangerous – able or likely to cause harm or injury.

environment – nature and everything in it, such as the land, sea, and air.

fossil fuel – a fuel formed in Earth from the remains of plants or animals. Coal, oil, and natural gas are fossil fuels.

generator – a machine that creates electricity.

habitat – the area or environment where a person or animal usually lives.

industry – a group of businesses that provide a particular product or service.

negative – having more electrons than protons.

positive – having more protons than electrons.

react – to change when mixed with another chemical or substance.

research – to find out more about something.

resource – something that is usable or valuable.

restore – to make something like it used to be.